Dum

Through the Lens
Glimpses of old
Kirkdale School, Carsluith

with notes by
Joan Mitchell

Dumfries and Galloway
Libraries, Information and Archives
2003

First published 2003
© Publication copyright Dumfries and Galloway Council.
© Text copyright Joan Mitchell.

Designed by Dumfries and Galloway Libraries, Information
and Archives. Set and printed by Solway Offset Services,
Catherinefield Industrial Estate, Dumfries for the publisher.

Dumfries and Galloway Libraries, Information and Archives
Central Support Unit, Catherine Street
Dumfries DG1 1JB
Tel: 01387 252070   Fax: 01387 260294
www.dumgal.gov.uk/lia

ISBN 0 946280 64 9
Kirkdale School, Carsluith is number 25 in the
Dumfries and Galloway: Through the Lens series.
For a full list of our publications contact us at the above address.

ACKNOWLEDGEMENTS

The material for this book has been supplied by
the former pupils and teachers of Kirkdale School
who provided the photographs and the memories.
The editor is very grateful for their patience and
enthusiasm as the project has taken some time to
come to fruition.

The major acknowledgement must however go to
George McCulloch and Janette Lupton who
conceived the idea for the school millennium
reunion and organised the event and the
collection of the material. Grateful thanks are also
due to Jimmy Dill for his generous contribution to
the costs of production and to Anne and Bren
McCarthy for their help and advice. Kirkdale
School logbooks were also a valuable source of
information.

The photo on the back cover has been kindly
provided by Mr Swain, King's Langley,
Hertfordshire.

Considerable efforts have been made to verify
facts, particularly names, but unfortunately there
are still a few gaps. The editor apologises for any
errors of fact or mis-spelling of names

Joan Mitchell

INTRODUCTION

Kirkdale School was opened on 11th August 1913 to serve the small village of Carsluith and its surrounding rural area. It replaced a school which had been established under the patronage of Miss Hannay of Kirkdale. This original school building was badly damaged by a quarry blast in 1939 but restored in the 1950s for use as the village hall.

The economic life of the community served by Kirkdale School revolved around farming, quarrying, and salmon fishing. Originating as a station for changing horses in the days of coaching, Carsluith grew with the granite quarries of the nineteenth century. Two small terraces, Waterloo Terrace on the shore and the Bayview Terrace ('The Raw') housed quarry workers. The character of the small village owed much to its location on the shores of Wigtown Bay. At Burnfoot, the Barr Quay was linked by tramway (known locally as 'the rails') to the Bagbie Quarry, and a fishhouse served Carsluith's other industry - the salmon stake nets.

Kirkdale School educated the children of Carsluith and district for 51 years, closing in 1964, when the remaining children transferred to Creetown school. For most of this time it was a two-teacher school, with Mr McKechnie as the first headteacher and Mrs McGill the last. Its decline in numbers in the late 1950s which resulted in its drop to single-teacher status and its eventual closure, reflected the decline in the numbers of farm children and dwindling family sizes.

In November 1999, former pupils of Kirkdale School, at the inspiration of George McCulloch, met in Carsluith Village Hall for a millennium reunion. A simple idea, it turned into a remarkable event with a hundred former pupils and partners returning from all over the World, including Taiwan, Australia and Seattle, USA. A notable highlight was the reunion of the seven members of the Dill family who had not met for 30 years and who were unaware that they were all going to be present. Guests of honour were former teachers, Mr Roy and Mrs Rae, both in their nineties.

The pupils brought their photographs and their written memories. These have been used to compile this booklet. The reminiscences of outside lavvies, the tawse, school concerts, coal fires, long country journeys on foot, playground games, friendships and fights, give a flavour of rural school life in Galloway in the middle years of the twentieth century.

Thanks are due to the organising committee of George McCulloch, Janette Lupton and Joan Mitchell, Jimmy Dill for his generosity, and Carsluith Hall Committee who hosted the reunion.

CARSLUITH VILLAGE
The main road through Carsluith (A75) in the quieter era before the First World War - looking south to the bridge over Carsluith Burn. The building on the left is the pre-1913 school, now the village hall, beyond which are cottages destroyed in the quarry blast, on 8th December, 1939.

CARSLUITH VILLAGE
The main road through the village at the bridge over Carsluith Burn looking north - obviously a good place to enjoy a gossip. The cottages in the right foreground were once the old coaching inn. Beyond the bridge are the cottages destroyed in the 'big blast', now the site of the car-park for the village hall, and the original school building. The photograph probably dates from the late 1930s.

BURNFOOT

Burnfoot from the Barr Quay promontory. The small houses on the left were fishermen's cottages. The substantial granite houses on the right were built in the first decade of the twentieth century. Their construction suggests a degree of prosperity, probably associated with the quarries, and an appreciation of an attractive shore site with the White Hill in the background.

BURNFOOT
Burnfoot on an important social occasion. Unfortunately the reason for this social gathering is obscure but it appears quite formal. The pathway in front of the houses provided access to the salmon stake nets beyond the Burnfoot houses.

c.1926 CLASS
Back row:- Mr Robert Watson (Headmaster), Willie Milligan, James Dickson, Roy Beattie, Adam Scott, Willie Hyslop, John Nish.
Third row:- Alex McGuffie, Tom Wilson, Peggy Nish, Jean Thompson, Jean McKie, Anna Smith, Mary Thompson, Jane Wilson, Lawrence Smith, Lex McGuffie.
Second row:- Marjory Christie, Jessie Wilson, Betty Bowman, Annie Wilson, Margaret Thompson, Ena Lupton, Jessie Johnstone, Effie Henry, Jean Baxter.
Front row:- Jim McGuffie, Peter Hyslop, John Smith, Anton McGuffie, David Johnstone, unknown.

MEMORIES

"Wet coats in the cloakrooms on a rainy day
Building lean-to huts in the Mill field
'Cake pudding' at school dinners
Fights at the Mill road end."

Anne McCarthy (Bowman) (mid 1940s)

"I remember Mrs Rae putting us round the fire (in what we called the Primary Class) during the cold winter mornings and our outings to the Campers' Green at Kirkdale and swimming at the Weir."

Robert Ross (late 1940s)

"Small bottles of milk, hot in summer, freezing in winter (sometimes the birds got there first)
Snow so deep in 1947 that you could only see the triangular top of the school sign"

Drew Kerr (mid-1940s)

"Playing wee hoosies up on the banking
Mum bringing me down from Bagbie with my boxes of rosehips I had gathered
Rev McEachern bringing puppets."

Elizabeth Houston (McKnight) (late 1950s)

1935 CLASS
Back row:- Mr William Benzies (Headmaster), Samuel Rae, ? Crawford, George Winchester, Anton Welsh, Willie Milligan, Willie Gordon, Murray Niven, Ian McGuffie, Billy Christie, Miss Marjorie Henderson (Teacher).
Third row:- Sadie Farrell, Nancy Whyte, Nellie Hyslop, Lily Johnstone, Belle McKie, Marjory Baxter, Nettie Welsh, Minnie Wilson, Helen Whyte.
Second row:- Nan Wilson, ? Crawford, Agnes Baxter, Maisie Hyslop, Edie Nichol.
    Front row: Jamie Nichol, Ed Flynn, Goerge Bowman, Willie Nichol, Jack Kerr.

LESSONS

Pupils' recollections remind us of changes in teaching techniques.

"What I remember about my time at school was learning things by rote: tables, spelling, main towns and rivers around Scotland eg Lerwick, Kirkwall, Thurso, Wick, Dingwall etc right round the country up to Oban. The rivers started off - the Dee, the Don, the Deveron, the Findhorn and Spey. To this day, sixty years on, I can still count and spell reasonably well and pinpoint roughly the area of Scotland where the main rivers and towns are situated - thanks to this, now not politically correct, form of education"

Marguerite Simpson (Parker) (late 1930s)

"The difficulty of dividing £26 13s 4d by 39 (long division). How many of today's youngsters could handle this?"

Drew Kerr (mid 1940s)

"The senior class is now working compound proportion sums".

School Logbook (March 1916)

"Slates are not now being used in school as the Authority has supplied a sufficient quantity of jotters to do for a long time."

School Logbook (November 1919)

1938 CLASS
Back row:- unknown, Norman McGuffie, John Christie, unknown, unknown, George Bowman, Jack Kerr, Jim Nichol, Miss Scrimgeour.
Third row:- Peggy Henry, Maisie Hyslop, Nettie Welsh, Helen Whyte, ? Farrell.
Second row:- unknown, Eleanor Nichol, Bertha Whyte, May Nish, Gertie Niven, Edie Nichol, Doreen Kerr, I Hope.
Front row:- unknown, Davie Hyslop.

FUN AND GAMES

Many pupils, from all eras, recalled the fun of playing 'up the bank' - the school playground included a grassy bank with a rock outcrop ideal for imaginative games.

"Digging for pignuts up on the bank and eating them.
Waiting at the dyke, by Hazelwood, for Major or Mrs Ewing to bring Oonah, their monkey to see us"
Peggy Lessey (Henry) (late 1930s)

"I remember playing rounders and the ball always ending up lost in the long grass on the banking.
The game was stopped till the ball was found because it was the only one we had.
Also playing with the click and gird"
Len Niven (1940s)

"At playtime we had seasons for skipping, hop beds and marbles and in the autumn we had the chestnuts"
Jessie Warren (Kerr) (early 1940s)

LIBRARY VAN
This cheery photo captures the anticipation of pupils unloading their new crate of books from the library van in the mid 1940s.

WAR YEARS

The war years seem to have ended class photos for a time but the written memories of pupils of the time are vivid.

"I attended the school during the war years. My first memories are of fires in the school and big kettles which were boiled on the fire and cocoa made at lunch time. Many people from the far out farms had to walk three miles to the school, so brought a lunch box. Once a month we would go to the post office and spend our sweet rations. "

Jessie Warren (Kerr) (early 1940s)

"I remember while out playing we would hear the army tanks coming, and we would all run to the hedge, and the soldiers would throw us packets of chewing gum"

Agnes McCulloch (Welsh) (mid 1940s)

"The arrival of Glasgow evacuees in early 1940s with Glasgow teachers. I remember particularly Miss Shanks - she could throw a duster (hard back) from ten yards and hit you without raising her head. In spite of the war I remember happy times with Glasgow pupils who always seemed full of life"

Tommy Christie (early 1940s)

"The children were told that the rule requiring them to carry their respirators each day to school had been changed and that in future they would bring them for inspection and practice on the first Monday of each month."

School Logbook (August 1942)

KIRKDALE HOUSE MAYPOLE
Children dancing round the maypole at Kirkdale House on an Empire Day outing, probably in the late 1930s.

SPORTS AND PICNICS

Outings to Kirkdale House and local picnics were fun days for pupils and provide some of the earliest memories.

"I remember sports at Ravenshall. Col Hannay would throw the money up in the air and the first to run the length of the field got the most money. In particular Jean Dill was a great runner. She always got the most"

Roy Beattie (1920s)

"I always remember the 24th May (Empire Day) and the sports in front of Kirkdale House with lots of lemonade and ice cream"

Billy Welsh (late 1940s)

"I remember our Empire Day outing. Each year the older girls were allowed to assist Mrs Rae and Mrs Whyte to make up the 'goodie bags', one for each pupil filled with sandwiches, shortbread and an iced bun. These were placed in a clothes basket for the older boys to carry. We all assembled at the gate, then marched in pairs the three miles to Kirkdale.
Along the way we sang marching songs. We ran races and played games in front of the big house.
Then the goodie bags were handed out with home-made lemonade from the house kitchen."

Janette Lupton (Parker) (mid 1940s)

15

OUTING TO EDINBURGH
In Summer 1949, school pupils visited Edinburgh Zoo.
Back row:- Anne Bowman, Netta Ruxton, Isobel Dill, Sandra McLean.
Middle row:- David Ruxton, Ian Little, Billy Thom, Tom Parker, Billy Welsh, Drew Kerr, Margaret Ross.
Front row:- Joyce Bowman, Jean Nichol, Elsie Kerr, Billy Watson, Ian Niven.

TRIPS AND TREATS

Even as early as 1938 teachers were taking pupils on ambitious trips which were much appreciated.

"I have good memories of going the school trip by train to the Empire Exhibition, Bellahouston Park,
Glasgow in 1938 and having lunch on the train"
Robert Kellie (late 1930s)

"I remember the school trip to Glasgow and the sail 'doon the watter' with Mr Roy who was a great headmaster,
full of kindness and who always taught us with great consideration".
Betty Gibson (Kellie) (mid 1940s)

"Trip to Edinburgh Zoo - in Smith's bus."
Drew Kerr (mid 1940s)

"I remember Coronation Day at Kirkdale School. The school held a sports day in the field behind the fish-house.
Every pupil was presented with a Coronation mug to commemorate the Queen's Coronation."
Alex Baxter (early 1950s)

"It was Spring 1953. Everybody was high on the excitement generated by the Coronation. Our family moved north. Names had
been collected at school for souvenir mugs etc. and these arrived after we departed. At our new school names had been collected
before we arrived. Missed out at both ends."
Joan and Sandy Lindsay (early 1950s)

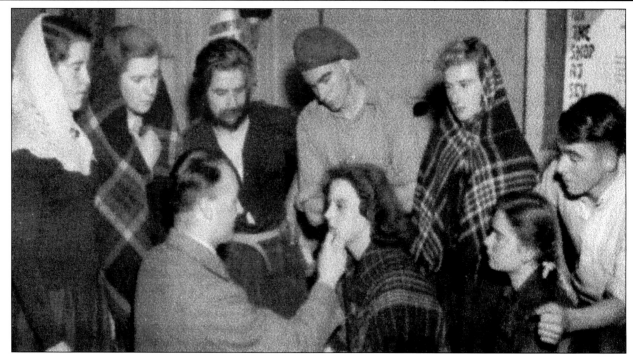

MR ROY AND THE DRAMA CLUB
In 1945 Mr Roy started both a Kirkdale Drama Club and a Kirkdale Youth Club.
Back row:- Isobel Whyte, Sheila Kerr, Pat Millar, Jack Kerr, Edie Nichol, Jackie Fisher.
Front row:- Mr Roy, Marguerite Parker, Betty Kellie.

PERFORMING PUPILS

School concerts were a regular feature of school life, and one which obviously left mixed memories!

"Taking part in the school Christmas concert dressed as Narcissus. When the curtain went up I fainted.
Kirkdale School was a great place to be. Mr Roy was a great headmaster."
Billy Watson (mid-1940s)

"The concert is on Wednesday. The stage was put up at the weekend.
We were doing the play 'The Knave of Hearts' with Miss Robertson today"
Extract from diary Joan Mitchell (Bowman) (1950)

"Walking to hall for concert and falling on steps up to stage dropping my baby (doll) as I fell."
Elizabeth Houston (McKnight) (late 1950s)

PRINCE GEORGE'S DRAGON
In 1951 the school put on *Prince George's Dragon* with Tommy Watson, Joan Bowman, Catherine Millar, Alex Baxter, Jimmy Dill, Hazel Nichol, Billy Thom (the King), George McCulloch, Evelyn McLean (the Queen), Alison Kerr, Margaret Dill, Robert McWilliam, Dougie Ruxton, Jim McCulloch.

CONCERT PROGRAMME

A MAYTIME MISCELLANY
by PUPILS of KIRKDALE SCHOOL
Friday 25th May 1951 at 7.30 p.m.
Chairman – Rev. John Good

PROGRAMME

1.	Psalm Tune	Kedron	School Choir
2.	Recitation	Dandie	Robert Weir
3.	(a)	Oats and Beans	Infants
	(b)	Vespers	Infants
4.	Play	Prince George's Dragon	Seniors
5.	Piano Solo		Robert Weir
6.	Verse Speaking		Seniors
7.	(a)	O' can ye sew cushions.	
	(b)	Rise, rise, thou merry lark!	Senior Choir
	(c)	Come, see where golden hearted Spring	

INTERVAL

1.	Play	Oh! Christina	Joyce Bowman
			Dorothy Johnstone
2.	(a)	Lucy Locket	Infants
	(b)	Lavender's Blue	Infants
3.	Play	Fish Queue	Seniors
4.	Piano Solo		Alison Kerr
5.	(a)	I will go	
	(b)	Schubert's Cradle Song	Senior Choir
	(c)	Bonnie Gallowa'	
6.	Song Scene	Rendez-vous	Seniors
7.	Rimington		School Choir

NATIONAL ANTHEM

21

EARLY 1950s CLASS (WEE ROOM)
Back row:- Miss Robertson, ? McGhie, Doug McCulloch, Andy Watson, Ian McConchie, Jim McCrindle (?), ? Turner (?).
Third row: Bruce Doak, Malcolm McLean, Billy Doak, Edmond Crutchfield, Watson Fisher.
Second row: Philip King, Joy Lindsay, Alison Millar, Margaret Weir, Irene Dill, Winnie McCulloch.
Front row:- Alan Turner, Jim Watson, Ronnie McCulloch, Kerr McConchie, Jock Watson.

FUN AND GAMES (2)

In 1950s still playing on the bank and eating pignuts!

"My memory of the school is about the freedom we had in those days - all the space in the playground which was unplanned and the games we played like kick-the-can invented by Drew McCulloch"

Angus Crutchfield (late 1950s)

"I used to run round the bank with a piece of wood in my hand thinking we were racing drivers against Bruce Doak"

Ronnie McCulloch (early 1950s)

"Digging up (and eating) pignuts!
Playing 'wee hoosies' on the rocky outcrop on the playground"

Jennifer Wilcock (King) (early 1950s)

23

EARLY 1950s CLASS ('BIG ROOM')
Back row:- Mr Weir, Jock Gibson, Jim McCulloch, Eric Johnstone, Henry Gibson, Robert Weir, Douglas Ruxton, Alex Baxter.
Third row:- Isla Ross, Margaret Dill, Robert Ross, Alan Walker, Sandy Patterson, Robert McWilliam, Mary Watson, Carol Anderson.
Second row:- Joan Bowman, Dorothy Johnstone, Evelyn McLean, Alison Kerr, Irene Doak, Jean Watson, Catherine Millar.
Front row:- Tommy Watson, George McCulloch, Jimmy Dill, Jennifer King.

PRANKS AND PUNISHMENTS

School life was not always a bed of roses. The belt or tawse features in several recollections, the playground teasing, and for many, the annual ritual of stealing Carsluith Farm pears.

"The mention of Kirkdale School reminds me of how I tried all the tricks in the book ie sore tummy, toothache etc to avoid going to school until one day the castor oil was produced and I had to decide between oil or school. School was the easier medicine."

Tom Parker (mid 1940s)

"Getting the 'tawse' for getting back to school late at lunchtime from Ackie Kerr's pear tree."

Malcolm Mclean (early 1950s)

I remember being 'put out' in the corridor nearly every day by Mrs Rae for laughing in class with Minnie McLean.

Betty Gibson (Kellie) (mid 1940s)

"Belly ache after dinner time raids on Carsluith Farm pear tree and Hazelwood Cottage gooseberry bushes"

Anne McCarthy (Bowman) (late 1940s)

"First time wearing glasses and being called 'specky' and 'four eyes'."

Mabel Martin (Watson) (late 1950s)

c1957 CLASS

Miss Parsons with back row:- Eleanor McConchie, Violet Dill, Mabel Watson, Drew McCulloch, Jennifer McCracken, George Watson, Wilma Winchester.

Front row:- George Hyslop, Peter Hyslop, Agnes McWilliam, Stewart Ross, Irene Dill, Winnie McCulloch.

PRANKS AND PUNISHMENTS (2)

Carsluith youngsters clearly demonstrated a lot of initiative if sometimes misdirected!

"My lasting memory is of the headmaster turning up at Auchenlarie to find the belt behind an oil tank,
stolen and hidden by my older brother, Ronnie."

Mary Cowan (McCulloch) (mid 1950s)

"I can remember the day Catherine, myself and two others decided to explore the lofts of the school. Two went up the loft and
two as look-outs. We shouted there was someone coming but they couldn't hear us so we were caught."

Alison Twiname (Millar) (early 1950s)

"Having 'segs' in the soles of my shoes and being told off for making too much noise when I walked across the room. As I was in
the infants I had to wait till Dad picked me up, so I was disturbing the 'big class' with my noisy feet"

Shona McClymont (Watson) (early 1960s)

"I used to get sent out to weed the playground because I couldn't sing (and so, of course, I still can't sing!) and I used to get the
belt for 'careless spelling' (and I still can't spell!!)"

Angus Crutchfield (late 1950s)

EARLY 1960s CLASS
Back row:- Mrs McGill, Elizabeth McKnight, Wilma Winchester, Janette Crosbie, Eleanor McConchie, Mabel Watson, Mr Boreland.
Middle row:- Stewart McKie, Patricia McKie, Janette Marshall, Andrew McKnight, Drew McCulloch, Andrew Reed, Janice Paterson, Sadie Marshall, Alan Paterson.
Front row:- William McKnight, Jim Nichol, Agnes McCulloch, Muriel McKie, John Winchester, Hughie Marshall, Jim Wilson, Mary McCulloch, Roma Nichol, Jonathan Crutchfield, Billy Nichol.

INTO THE SIXTIES

"Dear Mrs McGill She taught me the "3Rs" so well! I am indebted"
Jonathan Crutchfield (early 1960s)

"Watching the ink dry on the jotters of P7 as the sun streamed through the windows.
I longed to be old enough to use one of those pens.
When my turn came I could only make ink blots but with Mr Boreland's help I soon managed."
Janette Marshall (early 1960s)

"Kirkdale School opened today for the last time. Mr Laird and Mr Baillie called and took farewell of the children and staff."
School Logbook 23rd December, 1964

REUNION, 1999
Mr Roy (headteacher 1945-50), Mrs Roy and Mrs Rae (teacher 1945-48) (centre), all nonagenarians at the reunion in 1999.

THE DILL FAMILY
The Dill family - Robert, Isobel, Margaret, Jimmy, Irene, Violet and Elizabeth. One of the highlights of the 1999 reunion was the reunion of the Dill family, together for the first time in many years, with Jimmy coming over unannounced from Australia.

REUNION
Studying the photos and memories which have formed the basis of this booklet at the Millennium Reunion, November 1999.

REUNION
Old acquaintances renewed in Carsluith Village Hall at the Reunion in November 1999.

HEADTEACHERS

William McKechnie	–	1913-1919
Robert Watson	–	1919-1932
Mr Turner	–	1932-1934
William Benzies	–	1934-1945
William Roy	–	1945-1950
James P Weir	–	1950-1955
Robert H Hamilton	–	1955-1959
James Boreland	–	1959-1962
Mrs Mary McGill	–	1962-1964 (Single teacher)

ASSISTANT TEACHERS

Mrs Catherine McKechnie	–	1913-1914
Miss Mary Scott	–	1914-1916
Mrs Catherine Ann Wallace	–	1916-1923
Miss Johnston	–	1923-1925
Miss Marjorie Henderson	–	1925-1935
Miss Helen M Scrimgeour	–	1936-1937
Miss Hawthorn	–	1937-1939
Mrs Margaret McGuffie/Mrs Setz	–	1939-1945
Mrs Lizzie Rae	–	1945-1948
Miss May McGuffie	–	1949-1950
Miss Mhara Robertson	–	1950-1955
Miss Barbara Parsons	–	1956-1958
Miss Maureen Cronie	–	1958-1959
Mrs McGill	–	1959-1962